Previous Works

"Pages Torn From A Plague..."

RELENTLESS LIMINALITY

(a few collections)

STEVEN M. WUEBKER

BALBOA.PRESS

A DIVISION OF HAY HOUSE

Balboa Press books may be ordered through booksellers or by contacting:

Balboa Press
A Division of Hay House
1663 Liberty Drive
Bloomington, IN 47403
www.balboapress.com
844-682-1282

Print information available on the last page.

ISBN: 979-8-7652-4746-4 (sc)
ISBN: 979-8-7652-4745-7 (hc)
ISBN: 979-8-7652-4747-1 (e)

Library of Congress Control Number: 2023922062

Balboa Press rev. date: 02/02/2024

Dedication

To my husband, Joel.

Not this once, not this always...but for forever, I love you.

Contents

1. Relentless

2. The Papers

Part 1: The Paris Papers

Part 2: The Mexico Papers

3. In A City Of Men

4. One Last One

Preface

The preface for this book would be...my previous book.

Only because it became a reality first.

While the memories of that roller coaster ride through history may never abate, there is no reason to believe the ride ever stopped.

These new twists and turns burst through even bigger boundaries, even if it's only those shielding our mind's eye.

Always remember, "It's all about perspective..." – S.W.

Definition

"Liminality"

Liminality is a term used to describe the psychological process of transitioning across boundaries and borders.

The term "limen" comes from the Latin for threshold; it is literally the threshold separating one space from another.

It is the place in the wall where people move from one room to another...

Source: Google

1
RELENTLESS

Slamming her glass onto the table,
all that she could say was

"Bullshit!"

and as the candlelight
shimmered in her eyes,
all that I could see was emptiness.

"It's over then?", I asked,
feeling the hatred starting to flow.

And as she just stared,
all of the memories started
draining down my face.

"Last call...", the bartender said,
killing the front lights.
Yeah, I thought,
last call for love.

As her eyes searched mine,
I said,

"Thanks, it was fun..."

and blew out the candle.

"Untitled"

The monolithic face on Mars
most of us have seen it
      dusted in a charcoal-covered veil
      one not much different than those worn
          in funeral marches of yore
          ladies of the mourning
              sometimes even mourning
              ladies of the evening.

A blushing bride's armament
      the lace veiling secrets well
      much like a railcar's drawn shade
          only a bridal procession
          is much slower to pass.

We wander the recesses of our minds
      our anxieties moving boulders
      from in front of veiled caves
          other times, sealing them shut
          when even lifting a pebble
          is the day's only ominous task.

We used to be quick to tip our hats
      even remove them
      if presences warranted
          yet we have never learned to easily
          vail our veils...even after all these years,
              pebbles and stones be damned.

"Veils"

Candy that tastes of Christmas
        anise-flavored and everybody dreads

            "shit...it's that flavor again..."

you think
as those taste buds awaken.

The festive wrappers, green and red,
always greet one's sweet tooth

        (we eat with our mind's eye first)

before the ever-lingering guests of bad taste
will never retreat, over-staying their welcome
long after the coffee has been served.

"Hard tack"...the relatives remind you every year
        their memories are steadfast
        on some mental corkboard,
        holding tightly to a cerebral bedroom wall
        you thought you left from...a long time ago.

The anticipation, realization, and deflation
of getting one's hopes up

        unwrapping that mystery piece
        tossing the cellophane that never creases
        wishing and hoping

about gifts on Christmas morning...

Candy can sometimes be like that.

"Hard Tack'd"

It's like being back in college
       (that "sploof" tube)
dryer sheets stuffed
into the end of a cardboard tube
       softening the odors, or so we thought
       as we wrinkled our noses
       at the dankness of it all
hidden somewhere
in the bathroom cabinet
always ready to mask the smell
so no one knows you smoke weed.

Stuffing new sheets
       into a new tube
that scent takes you back
to college-dorm days, sunny afternoons
spent with friends, beside windows
       making mortal clouds
       that always stay so close to Earth
blowing "That's a huge hit, man!" phrases
through the stuffed tube,
coughing and trying to hide it
while telling yourself
these are the memories
you will remember
on a day
just like today.

Yeah...that old scent of dryer sheets.

"Sploof Memories"

The smell of butterscotch on the morning air.

I remember the old man...
he used to give me butterscotch candy
after he was finished playing "the game".
I can still remember the cabin
somewhere deep within the woods
of southeastern Michigan.
He used to take me there in the summer times,
"in the fun times" as he called it,
to play his game.
He is gone now,
passed on and paying his penance,
his price for having played the game.

The healing process is over now,
I am whole again.
Still I wonder...would he come back again,
invite me into the woods again,
consider me a player in his sordid game again?

How many others I do not know...
some of them have moved on as well,
seeking their therapy through death
because it seemed so much more of an escape,
so much better than the memories
of those woods and that damn cabin.

The cool summer evenings sometimes haunt me,
but my dreams are so much safer now...
knowing that, in the end,
the old man lost the game.

"Mr. Butterscotch Man"

I've never been into "gods", really...

Have you?

I mean, there's just so many;

lords, titans, ghosts – some holy

deities, incarnations, carnates

immortals, spirits, beings – some supreme

talismans, totems, icons, and more.

Take your pick! Any one of them!

Like winning at the balloon-pop
        carnival game with your last dart,
        the pickings may be slim or small
        but hey, at least you got to pick!

One never intends to find salvation
        at a traveling sideshow...

Games of chance...risking some eternality
by popping the wrong balloon.

Because to the right balloon,
it is the only one that matters.
        That wins.
        That salvation.
        That one chosen balloon.
        That god.

Take care that your aim is always centered,
regardless of which balloon you choose.

"Popping balloons"

On any given hotel elevator

  sometimes after "midnight-a.m."
    other times, after "mid-morning p.m."

there's always that random chance
a perfect trifecta will emerge

  perfect
  because you always remember
  old times smelling of the same

  long-ago memories
  some that strive to remain hidden,
  others begging to be embellished again.

Sometimes
a passing salesclerk
advertising their starring role
in a current remake of
"Three Martini Lunch"
  foisting remnant fragrances
  of ash-laden smoke breaks
  upon unsuspecting window shoppers,
  proof 100s will never be replaced
  or go out of style...an under-study
  "vape" will never win awards.

Other times
upon a lover's collar
straying from afar
      so many business trips
one only knows the telltale scents
because they too have adorned
those fragrant garments themselves
      once, or too many times.

That trifecta.
Sweet. Floral. Thick.
Enticing.

"Cigarettes. Booze. Perfume."

Stepping out of the courthouse
into the frigid winter air,
I'm free. Finally free.

And as I descend
to the awaiting car,
each marble step
reminds me of you...

long drives home from work
incoming phone calls of dial tones
old excuses for being late, again
casual friends stopping in restaurants
trips to the store, returns empty-handed
calls back home while on vacation

Why could I not see?
Love isn't that blind...

As the cold wind chills me,
I hear you calling my name

"Michael...wait....."

from the top of the steps.

Climbing into the car,
I don't look back.
I can't.

I am not the enemy here...

"A Day of Divorce"

I always used to show up half a bottle in
        never uninvited
        but not invited as much, often.

Drunks always gather
in flocks together at functions...
safety in numbers, my ass.
        Never at a Saturday evening worship service though,
        we don't like silence.
We're just more fun in groups
...or so we thought.

A drunk will never call another drunk
        "a drunk"
in public...it's an untapped code
so to speak.

But we always know
our own brethren and sistren's
watery, red eyes are from the joys
of reuniting again with eyedrops in tow
...or so we thought.

All the thoughts said aloud
        and the "saids" that should
        remain only thoughts
never a megaphone needed,
a drunk always uses
their inside voice...
        sober and otherwise.

The mornings after
eventually become one long day into the next long day after the
day-long hangovers
that are for amateurs
and bloody mary's
are not only for mornings
because
"a day without a buzz...never was!"
said some old hippie, sometime.

It's always alcohol-o'clock somewhere...
        sober or otherwise.

"Showing up drunk"

On any summer sunny day
      a cumulous-cloud kind of day
      sometimes, if any at all

at any given pool, communal or local
friends and frenemies yet to be known
      among and gathered round
      cliques that never expire

the still-too-lukewarm
      sky mirror of water
wavering reflections
      of steamrolled marshmallows and undulating clouds
      if you've never had an acid flashback
a ceaseless day-lightshow among coteries and fireworks
      other days, just clouds...if any at all

the assemblage of required tanning
      lotions, oils, bodies, activities
laid out upon towels, new and old
spread among pool decks, hot concrete
always providing an instant hopscotch
seasonal ritual to the shade
      if any to be found

>>>>>

(continued)

radios play, airwaves vying
for airspace above
battlements of sunbathers
armored in little else but egos
and sunscreen, their scent
masked by "tropical coconut oils"
        always a natural-habitat smell
        worldwide
because somehow, we've all been to the tropics
at some point in our lives,
        if only in our dreams

somedays, the nacho cheese fries
and over-burnt hotdogs never
leave the summer-warmth comfort
of a paper plate; other days
seconds and thirds are a must
and always shared with friends
        the cliques must be fed

the monthly rags and required reading, tossed
haphazardly into canvas totes
that will long hold missing bookmarks
        because hell and high water both,
        neither will get read, ever

>>>>>

(continued)

the summer news cycle is but three months;
many headlines and breaking stories await,
broadcast above the radios, loud enough
for other competitors to well-hear;
news travels fast to friends and frenemies
        alike, if at all

eventually the day winds down, shade
encroaching the dwindling survivors'
islands of sanctuary, desertedness
setting in as factions depart,
the pool deck cooling off and cooling down
        the loudness of the heat
        having lost its voice
sending the bathing soldiers homeward
nurturing sun-drenched battle wounds
and bruised egos, already planning
the next day's action of attack

and as always with every retreat,
that final turn and last glance back
with a bright-smiled wave and shout,
        although the shade has finally overcome
        another day of air raids and occupations
the sun always gets in your eyes
even with sun-drenched hair
falling across your face.

(for Tarsha)

"Summer Pool"

Never meet your heroes

       some famous author
       that elusive chef
       the rock-metal-country-pop gods

          a lot of people say

"you'll be disappointed..."
"they're not like you think..."
"we're not fans anymore..."

          a lot of others will say...

People dream from young ages

       looking up to pedestals, holding
       perched imaginary icons
       who always rank far above
       their own mortal souls

          or so we used to say...

Can you even imagine
       one day...possibly...meeting...hoping...always
       never becoming a reality?

We all need dreams, we all need heroes...
maybe we just don't need to meet them.

"A life without heroes"

Even though we walk
in our father's shadow
our entire lives,
the journey ahead
is but ours alone.

Still...there will always be
that shadow-figure looking back,
silently nodding approval
and sweeping a hand forward,
signaling us to continue on
our successful journey,
that we have chosen the right path...

Just knowing that
always makes it so much easier
to take the next step.

"Father's Day"

Whatever letter-number you wore,
you were a hometown star
a hero in a one-sub-shop hometown
long before "hero" became name-droppable
like confetti at a homecoming game

Whatever field elevated your specialty,
wooden in the winter
grassy in the rest of the months thereafter
because they are the only ones
that mattered "to coach"

Whatever trophies upon the shelves,
dusty and donned with ribbons, both
accolades from the days when spotlights
shone not only in your eyes
but glared from them just as easily

Whatever grown up and graduated is now,
wondering if spelling really was all that important
so long ago, "college thoughts" diminished
as summer months became long-forgotten periods
of lessons never learned

Whatever married life begat,
the trials and tribulations of many
becoming "one" as a whole family unit grows
while the roar of spotlights dim, long forgotten
and not even supplanted by memories now

>>>>>

(continued)

Whatever "it's steady" car dealership job,
not really a dead-end because
even car sales turnaround too
as the lackluster glare of spotlights
still sell repeat customers the good ole days

"Still got them trophies?"
"How's your mom and dad?"
"The kids?"
"You were really something..."

Whatever you go back for every now and then,
special banquets or service-club appearances
on the fields or down marble hallways
even into the back corner of the attic
to pull on that old letter-number jersey
trying it on even though it is dusty
and will fit like hell...you do it still
because you will always be in the spotlight
even when there's no one home to judge

Whatever movies have been made,
the best starring role, time and over again
is in your weekend-memories-marathon
mentally looping your vicarious dreams
clamoring to be in the glare of the spotlights...

one more time
if only in your mind.

"Dreams of fields I never left"

Through a holler church's door
lies a portal to faith
      one so far beyond
      a simple handling of snakes
and trepidation
and fear unknown.

The lean-to appearance
isn't of imagination
      it's intended hinderance
      bars nary a soul
even the most curiosity-seeking ones
will eventually enter.

Parishioners, many
have bared witness
by the shine of a moon,
      only to have blamed their visions
      on spirits of a more fluid world.

Yes...a portal to more than wonderment
and the woods beyond
      reflective of souls
      both coming and long-gone
holding the secrets of the songs,
psalms and more, so long-ago sang...

"Symmetrical Psalms"

"Do not forget to put the art in culinary arts..." – Chef Randy

A simple, yeasty loaf
      maybe sliced, maybe not
      from your local grocer
      because we always do.

Tannish-brown crust
      maybe the color of grass
      gone dormant some drought
      some summer ago.

Brownish-tan and darker on the ends
      perhaps a memory the color
      of dad's old leather briefcase
      sometime ago.

When sliced, if still warm
      even if the house has already been sold
      it will sell again
fresh-baked
bread steam
rising to greet
the new owners, reminding them
of why this is now home
      again.

The crannies and nooks
just waiting for the butter
to go spelunking
     cave-like enough
     to create a cenote
     simply on the plate
slicing knives be damned.

(For Chef Randy)

"Bread: a poetic still life"

A paintbrush stroke
a certain musical note
a specific singer's voice
that icing on the cake
        looking nothing like surreal...

Where does inspiration come from?

Universal beauty surrounds
        even the blind man
        recently gone deaf;
        our memories will never escape us,
        even when our own minds sometimes do.

So memories...of the natural world.

What about hopes, dreams, and wishes?
Do they truly inspire us?
To do better, to be better...at what? By whom?

Is there ever a competition
between what comes first

        tears, blood, sweat

if inspiration never awakens?

Jumpstart your day before
        the morning java even brews.
That daily spark.

Inspiration.

"Questioning inspiration"

Let's start off by asking

"Born into the wrong family?"

most people have wondered it
at least once;
the rest lie about it,
among other things in life.
Not to digress...

One has to be careful
when correlating that Icarus-father-son thing...
the father flies too close to the son,
who flies too close to the sun;
conundrums ensue.

Even the most hardwood
of a family tree
is reduced to a spaghetti pile
with one single adoption notice.

Sitting on decades of universal barstools
missing most family reunions
neither preceding either
but sometimes both
chasing vices down rabbit holes
you did not even know existed
just so your current vices could have company
wondering...do I really belong?

To them?

>>>>>

(continued)

Meanwhile,
the world you were born into goes on spinning.

It's only when you realize counter-clockwise
can also go vertical...
        a marching start to the beat...
        drummers...different...all that.

Once you branch off and don't "be like them"
        because they like it simple
you start to wonder...
who am I really?

How and why I did *not* turn out like this
        ...or something like that?

The answers...
always lingering within the personal heresy
of your own beliefs
knowing
you'll always be a gleam in some god's eyeball
even if you don't want to be.

Who am I?
Really?

(For "someone")

"heretic advantage"

Who chose the universal color wheel?

Because sometimes, rebirth
in the springtime isn't always
pastels and shadows of gray.

Sometimes the black of Halloween
pervades the "lilac grapes"
and "hyacinth rains" – choices
      on the color swatches one pulls
      from their own season of changes.

Who decided the red and green
of December?

      Are they truly holiday colors?

      Or just bright spots
      among drab weeks on a calendar
      that seem forever to pass?

Colors of religion, those too...
have their own seasonal changes.

White always leads one to believe,
while black, once again, will always
symbolize death.

Because rebirth is sometimes dark...

"Spiritual Color Wheel"

A bottle of a fifth, or
  a fifth of a Xanax, or
    a pack-a-day of 100s, still

Three crossword puzzles a day, or
  daily horoscope readings of hope, or
    scratch-off lottery tickets, a thing

A book of thousand-year-old verses, or
  biblical hoarding of canned goods, or
    a lone-dragon needle-chaser, eternally

The plethora of sentences floating through
  your head on a daily basis
each word a parade float on its own,
an ongoing procession of tasks
  marching by, cadence be damned
and the end never being seen; it's relentless.

We try to dampen the cacophony,
the ever-present rattling of anxiety
we call "tinnitus"
  because it makes
  us feel better
  to label everything;
    "O.C.D. – here we go again!"
    actually C-D-O,
    because it's alphabetized.

But nothing ever truly dampens
  nor shades in rose-color
the realities of our mental visions
  no matter how hard we try...

"Contact lenses for the mind's eye"

When the city is socked in for days
        omnivorous clouds ready to pounce
        and devour
a piercing skyline
not its last victim to be.

San Francisco may have its bay
that banks the fog; Boston is
nothing like that, more so a haze
lingering from forgotten trials centuries ago.

Bewitching history among haunted trails
        freedom only for the tourists sprung
        from the daily shuttles to and fro
running amok among a city of ghosts
seeking their own freedoms, yet still
they have never left. Other maiden flowers
and voyages certainly never lasted this long.

In the old church cemetery, one walks
among the anciently-christened chariots
        daemons and phantasms perched atop sarcophagi
        watching the never-ending parade of gawkers
        more so than a La Tomatina non-participant
        above the fray and cacophony
long ago abandoned in a forever-search for peace.

No matter how many times one experiences it
        the smell of ocean water
        refreshing always
                not quite a slap in the face
                winter-brisk
        but enough of a knock
        to one's olfactory remembering
                to recognize
                that slightly salty air.

"Harboring in Boston"

We were not west coast-Hollywood
wealthy by any means
        but in a mid-western, fly-over state
        kind of wealth by measure
                as middle-classified wealth goes

We were offered a wealth of freedom
a mid-1980s teenage lifestyle
        a middle-class among classes;
        we were never "just average"
                we set our sights higher than most

We trespassed across hearts and minds
and truanted our souls for no reason
        our daily existences abounded
        unchecked - time and space, limitless;
                the parental concerns were busy middle-classing

We relished our middle-classism
always aware of shifting strata
        a level or two of movement either way
        the seismic shifts were always damaging
                even within our own subsets

We never paused for even a middle-second
clocks always ticking, judging
        the popularity of being more than
        "middle-fied" - future days be damned
                one always held higher aspirations, always

>>>>>

(continued)

We never in a middle-between years
imagined one day looking back
     such stations in life are always transitory
     across the middle, the divide, the spaces
          in the middle, always a passing phase

We carry our nostalgic memories
like patches from battlefields
     many have succumbed to unnecessary wars
     fought across the middle-classes
          the stratification scars will always remain

be wary of time
it knows no "middle"
only battle

and the end
will always arrive
from the front and the rear...

your classification rank be damned.

"Aspirations of nostalgic nihilism"

Whatever happened to the protagonist
in O. Henry's story
about a girl
    who waited for the artist
        to die painting a leaf
           before she realized
                her own self-worth?

Did she move on, herself
becoming a famous writer,
about nature perhaps,
in some offensive-handed way?

Did she become a painter, artistic
in her own beliefs, not only
about how she got better
but maybe *why* she got better;
religious iconography, her forte?

Did she become a mother,
raising an even sicker child, one
that not even a painted forest can
save, no matter how many artists
are felled?

Or maybe it was just a short story after all...

"Poetic Graffiti"

If burdens shared days

("*A month of Sundays!*")

centuries would become
the equivalent of a page-a-day calendar
        used and spent
        scattered about
        now scribble pads...full of doodles
to some.

"Weight-bearing load"
concerns not only
a task-master builder.

Shouldering one's own world
        and the accompanying moons, satellites, stars
often stresses the limits of joints unseen;
        psychic vortexes, bowing
        inward-outward
        weathering mental windstorms
                solar flares paling in comparison
        the universal center always being
        true north, and like magnets
        returning to stasis once again,
        exhausted.

"Atlas in repose"

Another moonrise across the desert
and the day's warmth, rising
embracing a nightfall
that will see me through my dreams,
once again.

How many others
        witnessed, witnessing now
have taken in, experienced
this nighttime wonder
        shared, sharing now
the same commonality of the sands
beneath my feet...

Time...it too passes
and sometimes invites memories along

...through our own hourglass
we must fall.

The vastness of the spaces
between grains of sand
        souls searching the universe
wondering if everything's separated
or so it seems...

"Moonrise on the desert"

Riding canyons of sandstone moons
that beckon of painted deserts

     astral streetlights lamp-lighting
     the way through journeys

sometimes barely colored
by pastel memories, other times
branding-iron amber

sears and chars across the landscape
     hashmarks across fine dining or fine memories
     either just another day's experience
         across an aridness that does not always blanket
         yet insulates the isolation even more.

>>>>>

(continued)

Illusionary sideshows and rodeos of the mind

     sometimes towering higher than these
     quarries and caverns I ceaselessly journey

some "cowboys" will hold on for much longer
than 8 seconds…
     months-days-years
sometimes even becoming lifetimes…

no matter how much the clowns antagonize,
getting "bucked off" would be the easy route
     shaking loose of the wild stallions
     that continually kick the stalls of barns
        and corridors of one's mental stables.

>>>>>

(continued)

Pulling rabbits out of hats
   flowers from a magic wand
     or never-ending tissues from a tuxedo sleeve...
     shooting stars that never proffer wishes
    starlit nights from universes past
  and moonbeams that will still burn...

showmanship always takes a three-ring circus
and all of the rings at once
to keep the "illusionistees" satiated and happy.

Center stages are for theaters
other than the mind...
    sometimes intermissions can be equated with nirvana
     even if it's only a 15-minute respite
     with blinking lights or pulsing stars
     bringing one back to their seat or saddle
     respectively...

>>>>>

(continued)

Mountains have been moving for expanses longer than eons
yet one's own attempt at moving mountains never ceases...

       horizons are never erased or grown closer;
       it's that illusionary thing again.

Perception.

Shadowed by majestic spires
       basilica pebbles and stones tossed about
              forces stronger than gravity
              can and do rain upwards.

There will always be cathedrals to be built
canyons to be explored
deceptions to be illuminated.

Unorthodox illusions, uncharted trails.

Magical.

It's showtime...

"Maverick-ician"

What would we talk about
        all those nights ago
after lights-out and your parents
had gone to bed?

A "tap-tap-tap" on the blinded windowpane
        sounding like a common raindrop
        if it were an excessive stalker
then the slow opening of the window
        your sheepish grin already wider
        than the gap between us – "Hey..."

and then hours later
        that were really only minutes
we'd both be on our ways
        you, back to your bed and dreams
        me, on to a night of paned-relief...from what I still do not know.

What would we talk about
and why could it not wait
until mornings after?

The moonlight only hushed our voices,
everything else
was as clear as the day at night....
back then.

"Midnight Windows"

All the world can be a stage
or something like that
        and always set the stage, they say

so imagine if you will
a small dock
        a pier of some sort
jutting out into some
random body of water
        a small pond, perhaps
        you've been there before
a small jetty, maybe
4-6 logs sunken deep on each side
        petrified planks making up a rickety dock
            spaced evenly across and apart
        just enough so to moor a small dinghy
for the evening.

Brown pillars sunken so deep
their treasures not beholden by chests,
but the trust the boat's ropes
place in them
for their nightly stays.

The water
shimmering deep greens,
darker darks, and almost some blues...
the moon is never known
for its color wheel.

The water will glisten
all thru the night's moonlight,
creating an aura of security
for both vessel and berth.

See, poetry can be descriptive
and detailed...if you take the time.

"Short piers are always good for long thoughts"

River queens, river kings...
river boys and girls

      there have already been
      millenarians upon generational millenarians
      to take their place
           at times, their tales already told
               taking up arms to save their river
                   closely, their secrets they hold

because it flows...the river
      through their livelihoods
      through their veins
it flows.

Family secrets
      buried deeper than catfish-mud
have traveled further through generations
than the river's length
      or any of its shores
upon which the mansion-plantation-estates
call home.

The term "dirty south" may not refer to secrets;
some question if it should.

Although "clean north"
      whatever that may mean
      wherever that may be
           hanging its laundry out to dry
           billowing in breezes only summer days can bring
still leaves the old stains of ages
that will always remain yellow.

River queens for river kings
      and the men they think they are...

"River Queens, River Kings"

Do you think a time traveler
ever gets tired of acclimating

      (reacclimating? reanimating? reincarnating?)

themselves
just to fit in
with the "in crowd" of the times?

How far does one have to travel
      to be considered a time traveler?
Travel is always measured in miles
      even though it should not always be.

Inward journeys are stationary
but the distance, it too is measured

      by "space.................apart"

even to the clairvoyant looking over their shoulder
while standing on the rim of an abyss.

Reanimating oneself so many times
over time
projecting animated sketches throughout our lives...
sometimes reality needs a break from us.

>>>>>

(continued)

Do you think anyone ever wishes
"Bon Voyage!"
to a time traveler
or
do we do it every day, every time
we say "Goodbye..."
as a loved one leaves for
                        work
                              play
                                    school
somewhere
away from us?

It's that "distance" thing again
        too-far or never-far-enough...
        aren't they the same really?
Especially if one can always reacclimate...

"We are all time travelers, aren't we?"

They say never burn bridges
        to save that for never
better yet to let the open road stay,
for the traveler will always lead themselves
to their own demise...

Short paths, long paths
                                        neither matter so

it's the journey with no exits
                                        to salvation
                                        to otherwise
that will become road tales
                                        legends made long ago...

Bridges are built for reasons
        more so than just common crossings
spanning lifetimes forged
in generational irons and bonds
        sometimes forgotten
        sometimes forsaken
strong enough to survive
any hell storm passed
or yet to come.

Burning bridges...never.

"The consequences of fire"

There is something about the seasons
     and its changes that makes us giddy.

Maybe there's a better choice of words....probably, yes.

But let's be plain and simply honest
     that slightest of shift in our internal, barometric pressure
     always gives us joy...

Giddiness.

That first hint of chill
     in a late summer morning
that first really warm day
     in an early spring

     ...a sole, fallen leaf
     ...a lone daffodil poking through

everything that reminds us

     "we are still alive!"

among
the bustles, the hustles
of our every days.

Winters never last as long as summers...
     we only think they do.

Telling ourselves, wishing and hoping
     the next season comes sooner than the previous
        even through all of the years
        as Mother Nature's orderly fashion
        seems intentionally neglected.

So yes,
wallow in the frivolity of the universe
while always remembering
that seasonal changes come but once a year.

And always, remember the giddiness...

"Autumn Giddiness"

Question of the day
     if you are one so inclined
     to think of those things

do the digital images we possess today
mean as much as the old adage implies...

     "a photograph...faded and folded...with yellowed corners..."

Are they placed in high regards
within the mental card catalog
of our universal psyche...

     take a child to any library
     give them a classic title
     then turn them loose
     within the Dewey Decimal System
          so much bigger, it will seem
          than their own solar system
          they will never forget

>>>>>

(continued)

would they view it as something so archaic
it cannot be believed?

Much like history taught us
about the gold miners of yore

knocking flint against steel
to secure their nightly fires
their daily rations of need

whereas today, our "MaRE"s
(meals ALMOST ready to eat)
are only a push-button start away
on a propane gas grill

why would anyone want to waste
their time
in a physical, non-digital world?

Eventually even mental photographs fade
(flint and steel, long ago parted ways)
because there will always be sparks
of digital imagery to keep us
too occupied and too distracted forward
to be that concerned about our pasts...

"Digital Memories"

A single bite into anything
    with even a hint of maple flavoring
    (syrup, frosting, candy)
and then
the sensation of being transported
back to that place of wonder,
of discovery, of the new-found
mental freedom when one first
discovers further places to roam;

Aullwood.

Annual fieldtrips through the years, seasonally
guiding elementary into junior high
    by then too old to appreciate it
    too old to even care about the loss
    of wonderment
the woods and paths to the farm
never changing except for age,
height, depth, color, and experience;
    okay...maybe changing a little.

Aullwood.

>>>>>

(continued)

The small red building.

The Audubon Center.

    Always dubbed "a museum"
        sometimes for the fragile minds
        and to make the youngerlings
        feel special, to feel the feels,
        and to remember that first bite
        of gritty, sugary candy that was sold there

    always smelled faintly of cedar boards,
        reminiscent of the many
        chests where our grandmothers
        kept their finest quilts,
        linens, embroidery, memories

    always a deep maroon color, often
        painted by our older siblings,
        sometimes due to detention,
        probation, or their realization
        of being an early tree-hugger.
        We all were "Trailblazers" once,
        at one time…if we were lucky.

Aullwood.

>>>>>

(continued)

There's no place like it…
    if you've been there once
    if you've been there year after year
    you know
because you remember
that grittiness, that sugary grittiness.

Every time…any time…
the first bite into some sugary-maple anything
and the rolling waves of memories come rushing
from so many years…reminding, "Yes. I'm back!"…

Aullwood.

"Aullwood. A Magical Place…(because we remember)"

Waiting is ironic.

Time passes
        too slow
        too fast
        no other way.

A diagnosis..and test results,
        our anxieties never matching the cadence of a pallbearer's
march
                too slow

A car crash that one did not see coming,
        telling ourselves to be better careful, we will be better careful
next time
                too fast

Only in an exact moment, there is no waiting.

Waiting
        too slow, too fast
it's never perfect.

"The ironies of waiting"

The air is different here,
        lighter somehow.
Magical.

So dry and arid
        even the mountains
        possess a scent
        ...if you listen long enough.
Mystical.

And if one is lucky enough to glance through
Mother Nature's bipolar keyhole
        seeing her coastal neurosis
                white, snow-capped mountains
                brown, sand-lined coasts
one may realize just how
grandiosely miniscule our
universal significance truly is.

Yet...
there will always be desert roses
        even if only sometimes immortalized in songs,
        their remembrances only as strong as the basin rocks
        holding and supporting the guardian mountains steadfast
sometimes though only in memories.

The sand that welcomes the ocean
and the snow that became the waves
        long-forgotten friends, reuniting
        in embraces of remembrances
        and miles journeyed
        only to suddenly part again
no different than
two time-travelers passing
in airport terminals
sometimes...with that same dry aridness
in the air.

"Bouquets from Coachella Valley"

Sunrise along the delta...somewhere.

The morning's warmth always a greeting
        "Southern and friendly!", always
        but always a tad thick and a bit guarded
the night's grasp long ago released
except for the heaviness it always wears.

The new day's warmth
        some mid-August, any Mid-South anywhere
humidity, not quite smothering
yet doting enough, a constant reminder
Mother Nature will never cut the apron strings
for any of her children; favoritism
is not an option.

>>>>>

(continued)

The warmth, the smells of the delta
        vaporizing itself; something else
        to linger with the humidity
                a travel companion for your
                day's journey

        not quite a rot; old cotton vines
        and water reeds, laid bedding
        along the shores
                in the delta
                everything's "a shore"
                or at least askew

        but a heaviness, if smells
                competed in weight classes
                        burnt popcorn being
                        the title holder

        a sense of old, that it's been here
                there, everywhere
                but settled here
        for a long time, for a lot of mornings.

>>>>>

(continued)

The delta sunrises...
       will always welcome one home
even those as transitory
as the waters creating its bogs.

Inhale deeply once again,
even though one needs no memory
of places once called home,
always.

"Sunrise on the Delta"

Airborne.

Taking the redeye.

                    North
        West
                              East
              South

The four directions do not matter.

There is a cross in each way
        maybe somehow promising a security
        that angel wings prove stronger than metal
yet between
a ton of feathers, a ton of steel
the metal tube always arrives at the final destination first
regardless of layovers or delays
        ...at least in our mind's eye.

The nighttime loftiness.

Edging closer to the heavens' ether,
not quite piercing the dreams we are made of...
        but far enough away from the Earth's binds
        so that post-midnight visions stream as seamlessly
        as the long-ago-ran entertainment available
        on the headrest in front of you.

>>>>>

(continued)

Neck-pillows, tray tables, drawn shades…
all acceptable bedding for a fly-over state sojourn through the darkness,
awakening in zones time never bothers

> in twilight or simply just zoned-out
> sleep overtaking some, pills or booze for the assist…
> others getting a jump start on a new working day

because time never waits for those who have no boarding pass.

Meanwhile this steel ton of feathers still circles, awaiting a clearance to land.

Early morning coffee quickly brews
while low cabin lights slowly rise
> and even though a sunset never occurred
> and a single moon was never found
somehow a new daylight has been crossed into
a new time zone already ticking away
an eternity of waiting for the late-risers to deplane
and find their direction
to find their final destination.

But regardless of the time of day or night…
flying is still hell.

"Taking the redeye"

I met you when we were young
across a babysitter's field of vision
two across many embodiments
soul-searching for friendships
many more than our single-digit ages,
so we hoped
              ...but you and I met.

I met you in the halls of friendship
schooling ourselves through middle ages
of life as we illusioned it,
knowing our fallacies ahead lay
only in the false love we shared,
so we hoped
              ...but you and I met.

I met you in a premonitory ocean of regret
knowing rebounds would be for more
than off the court, the field, the track
wherever it was you ran off to
away from the memories of our reality,
so we hoped
              ...but you and I met.

There have been many.
None better than the other.

"Multiple Muses"

Two strangers approach my door...

Him.
Youthful in an ageless kind of way
but not young.

>Polyester-everything
>tie, pants, shirt, personality;
>static.

Her.
Aged not in a youthful kind of way
but not young.

>Stringy-everything
>shawl, torn handbag, hair, eyes;
>inquisitive.

"WHAT DO YOU THINK OF THE BIBLE?"
said with such a glaze over their eyes.

That sheen...a kind that disturbs
even someone already in their grave.

Her.
Not saying anything, but everything, with her nods.

Him.
An orgiastic glee of non-poker-face emotions
escaping from his plastic "Action Figure for Jesus" grin.

Their level of internal climax
is barometrically off the dial
        measuring not the success of saving another soul
but the actual manifestation of the act itself
becoming a reality once again.

If addictions to religion are nothing more
than savior-overdoses from the
orgasmic shivers of proselytizing,
I may have just witnessed a holy ghost.

Maybe I should have saved them.

"Witnessing the orgasmic shivers of proselytizing"

Art is a manifestation
of an individual's perception
brought forth into the universe
for others to experience...

if they choose.

Not to be judged,
liked, or disliked;

simply for the experience itself.

"Describing art to an alien"

a new bicycle
money from the lottery
will she want to marry me someday

What do you wish for?
Hope for?

Always etched in the mental chambers
long maybe forgotten
until certain lights
cast the shadows
of memory aside,
once again revealing
a life unlived, a life
of hopes unrealized,
a life of simple cave drawings
and hopes and dreams that remain hidden
always.

What do you wish for?
Hope for?

Have you been spelunking lately?

"hieroglyphical hopes"

Some college course somewhere
some time ago
once proposed a concept...

about dreams.

What if our dreams are reversed
and whatever they are
at night in this world
is actually our true reality

and what we have come to know
as the real world
is actually only a dream.

Consider it.

Our nightmares are actually
our true reality,
yet we spend more of our
memorable waking hours
in this lifetime of dreams.

Why is that?

Because sometimes...it can be more terrifying than reality.

"Dreams in reverse"

Every summer, the memories of you...
still.

Into the wilds of nature, we escaped.

Long country road drives
through sun-drenched cornfields
        stopping along hidden bends
        in the road, sharing
        a joint; laughter.

Late-night strolls through the fairs,
seeing friends and the weather alike;
fair. Always.

A hidden smile, the gleam
        in your eyes and its meaning
        from across the beer tent,
                across from each other
        battling who will look away first;
        it was me. Always.

Funny how a summer garden puddle
        a delicate cistern collected
        among petals, pistils, and leaves
becomes a flower-petal-lake
and the memories floating to the top
        like jellyfish-stamen
        lurking below the surface
will always sting the same.

Every summer...still.

"On Petal Lake"

Flip the sign to closed
        and turning out the lights,
noticing one last clump of hair
        caught somehow in a corner-
it will still be there
        come morning.

The smells of old shaves and after spice;
        young men, old men
        all with their stories
                telling now or to be told
        but always...stories.

The news of the year
        always on and up for discussion
and remember
        there are always three sides
        to every story
        in the barbershop.

Friendships, fights
        flights of fright, sometimes
        for a little one's first trim
Rites of weddings, births, deaths, passages-
        and sometimes in that order
always fodder for thought, harvested
        from sacred grounds
        in the barbershop.

>>>>>

(continued)

From baby curls to furls
        of gray, time passes
quickly...marching alongside
the daily cadence of customers
passing thru
        town, then gone.
        tri-weekly, just a bit off the top.
Always welcome, welcome always
        as long as they bring
        a story to share
        in the barbershop.

And as the dust settles
through its evening's haze,
        the front signage long ago turned
the after spice and odd fritzes
settle into the empty chairs,
        taking up audience for
        long after the full moon's rise
so the stories
may continue to linger
        in the barbershop.

(for Joi)

"Barbershop"

"An end-of-lifer clinging daily
       to that last strand
       of universal lights,
hanging upon the eaves of life
       as sunset rapidly approaches
       that one last, still-twinkling bulb..."

Death is just the next chapter
       in the open book
       of our lives,
souls sometimes too afraid, hesitant
       to turn that page,
       to finally close that book.

Encyclopedias have been bound
       capturing pages thru the ages,
       reincarnating history. Again.
Stories of lifetimes have been tv-shown,
       played on outdated channels
       long ago set to repeat syndication.

Death...the number one best seller in everyone's lifetime.

"Writing Memoirs"

Do not mourn my death
for I was a soldier of my own fate.
I died with dignity, with pride.

I believed in what I was doing,
giving someone else what I have
had for so long.

I took pride in myself, my friends,
and above all, what I was doing.

I ask you, do not cry for my death,
but cry tears of joy, of happiness,
and of freedom.

I left behind a lot, I know,
and I'll never be replaced.
Yet, what my country gave to me
will never be forgotten.

I gave my life trying to give
my country's gift to someone else.
To myself, I ask, "What more
could I give for freedom?"

So now, I ask you, do not mourn
my death, but mourn for those
who have no freedom.

"Soldier"

Watering outdoor plants
        in a rain shower
                while listening to Radiohead

trying not to notice
        the dark cloud overhead
                wondering if it too has

a dark cloud hanging overhead
because eternity goes on forever,
correct?

"radio headphone showers"

low rivers never completely dry...
      hopes of past dreams never return...
          and addictions are reincarnatable...

"Another untitled piece"

2
THE PAPERS

Part 1

The Paris Papers

Brouillard sacre sur la terrain
(Sacred fog on the fields)

Until the last day
after forever,
I will continue searching
for you...
    so many days
    so many fields
    so many centuries
and still, so much fog...

Through the cities of lights
or over the coasts of darkness,
        one day
there will be a day
when you return to me...

Mon cœur
pauses quotidiennes,
attendant ton retour... perdu quelque part
parmi le brouillard sur les champs...

"Paris – 12/1/2017"

Paris
city of light
city of night
city of fright
city of might

Fear once patrolled
your streets.

Now, tourists
        wielding more power
        than atrocities ever could
control your avenues
        control your Metro
your Mona Lisa
        your tour Eiffel
                your "Palace de Whatever"
or at least they think they do.

Now, gentrification
everywhere taking over
what was once
a grand idea,
now old buildings becoming new,
now a city losing the luster
that once was an attraction.

Paris, take back your city…

"Paris #2 – 12/2/2017"

Winter through the trees...
why do they shed
their leaves in autumn
when they should be
bundling up for the cold?

The snow on the ground
        (a tree skirt, per chance?)
wintertime in Europe,
not quite the Christmas card of old
yet still picturesque
        in some old way...
                in some odd way...

Over the countryside,
through the woods and rivers,
bringing me somehow
somewhere
closer to you
again...

Winter in Europe
        darkness earlier
        than days before
I wrap my scarf
tighter,
I bundle up for
the cold,
awaiting spring
along with the trees...

"Winter In Europe"

I toil…

I toil thru the months
the seasons
the years
year by year
year after year
so many years…

Keeping watch
on the time
never a minute
to waste
never a second
to spare
I toil…

I toil to keep
the memories at bay,
no devil's work
for these busy hands
idle time
idle mind
not for these hands, not for this mind
I toil…

>>>>>

(continued)

The tick-tocks
of a daily
existence
these I never know
for I toil
      to keep the mind occupied
      to keep the mind at rest
rarely is there sleep
at night,
the memories
      they exist
keeping time
with the passing of it,
they are never far
from my dreams
I toil…

Life goes on
      as it always does
ticking and tocking
always…
like the hands
of another clock
always moving forward
to another day
to another memory…
why can't I?

For your memory,
I toil…

"The Maker of Time"

My ship has come in
     dry-docked on a beach
     somewhere within my mind…

High tides
will never set me free
     again…
My masts
will never hoist their sails
     again…

Anchors
     long ago, "aweigh-ed"
have settled into
the sands of time
     the sands of years past
leaving memories
tied to a low tide,
never to be washed away
again…

My ship…..

"Ship"

Your architecture
brings you to life...
  cobblestone streets
  centuries old
  the stories that have traveled
  across your paven path
what secrets of life
hide behind your facades?

What could we learn today
from the journeys of yesteryear,
from the many miles traveled,
wearing you down...day by day?

Jet-lagged tourists
with no clue
as to the many miles
you have witnessed,
of the many stories you have heard...

How many moons
how many suns
how many clouds
have crossed your path?

And I stand here,
wondering which way to go...
which way to go....

"Cobblestones"

An airport.

It doesn't get
any more anonymous
than that...
a hotel room,
maybe.

Travelers passing
        each other?
        time?
but always on the move.

Get in
sit down
buckle up
learn safety
but never talk to your neighbor.

An airport.
You can go...
        far, sometimes not far enough
but you can go...
        be a stranger in a stranger land
but you can go...
        just never talk to you neighbor.

An airport.

Fly the friendly skies.
Alone.
Anonymous.

"Anonymous Airlines"

Part 2

The Mexico Papers

A lone boat
a single fisherman
piloting back to sand
after guarding the shores
all night.

Sunrise
waking life back to
      the sand
      the palms
      the morning birds and their songs.
Still, the pier lights
blink on
never sleeping
never needing to rise and shine
      a warning for some
      a welcoming for most.

The sun is up now
the clouds are white again
      some god's morning marshmallows
no longer threatening
no longer a dark menace
to that lone fisherman
guarding the shores,
keeping us safe
from the waves of the night…

"Mexico – Day 1 – Sunrise"

Mayan gods
pulling back the lunar blanket from the ocean's surface
      protecting us
      from the creatures of the night
      exposing us
      to the creatures of the day

The lights from the island on the horizon
      twinkling in the distance
      like one last strand
      of Christmas lights
      that have yet to burn out,
      but are still hung upon the eave
waiting…
for the next guest to arrive
for the next holiday to come
and go.
Finally.

The solar orb
winking from behind a cloud
      some god's eyeball
      looking down,
      assessing the day
      as it begins
granting rays of approval
to come join in the revelry
that is life…
once again,
for another day.

"Mexico – Day 3 – Sunrise (again)"

Wouldn't it be awesome
to have seven days
on a beach
doing nothing
but just writing
and drinking, and writing, and eating, and writing?

But wait
I have already had many days
on that beach
and a little writing, and some eating, and a lot of drinking,
        but writing, not so much...

                And the waves
                keep crashing into shore
                reminding me
                just how far they
                have traveled,
                reminding me
                of their strength,
                of their power.
                Reminding me
                of just how much respect
                we owe the seas
                and the oceans.
                Reminding me
                of its depth
                of memories,
                and reminding me
                that it will
                keep on remembering
                long after I am gone,
                washing ashore
                my memories
                for someone else
                to find on the beach,
                alongside a seashell,
                reminding them

of just how far
they too have traveled.

But writing,
not so much…

"Mexico – Day 5 (hard to believe)"

Sometimes
it is really difficult
to be
an American
abroad....

(to be continued, sometime)

"To be continued..."

Mexico - Day 5 – Again.

5:47am tourists
walking through the resort
re-awakened zombies
     some stranded in a drunken haze
     after last night's last call
waiting
for their soul
to awaken,
waiting for their sun
to resume,
waiting for their day
to begin,
again.

Tourists
vacationing at the seaside
regimentally arising
marching towards their
regimented chaise lounges
striving to beat their
fellow commuters
for the best seat
     at the pool
     on the train
just like at home.

>>>>>

(continued)

Tourists
coming here to relax
telling themselves
they are
"getting away from it all…"
internal alarm clocks
behaving so much better here
than the ones left behind at home.
No snooze alarm here!

Yes!
Vacation!
Relax!
Commute!
Regiment!
Stress!
Retire!
Rest!
Resume the next day!
Again,
just like home…

"All-Inclusive (just like home)"

3
IN A CITY OF MEN

I have been here before
this edge of darkness
the city before sunrise
or just after sunset
puddles on the sidewalk
reflective of nothing
        but darkness.

Why do I live in the city?
I think it's for variety
the weirdos, derelicts, whores, drunks
all those people
who exist in my days
making me feel relatively sane again.

Seeing jesus eating french fries and a coney
or santa claus slouched in a wheelchair,
nothing shocks reality to life
like a day in the city.

But darkness
the type of soul one must have
to live here day-by-day
in a place
where happy hour is everyday
on every curb and corner,
sometimes I feel like a participant
in some eco-world experiment

        crazed scientists
        watching over me

gone awry....

"San-La-City, Somewhere"

(B. Cuente)

Decadence...debauchery
pain and suffering
tit-for-tat

the band has finally stopped
playing in the fields of love
and is waiting
      somewhere in the shadows
to be paid.....

(Jimmie Angel)

Cold
lonely
heart.

Lost
stolen
soul.

Siberia, I am.

"Unknown men"

The night was calm
the beer flatter than imaginable,
but still drinkable.
Then I ran into you.
Your smile lit up the night
as a lighthouse in a fog storm
sometimes does.
And as I grasped your hand
        (my eyes met yours)
our grips tightened and I felt it,
the knowing of an unknown bond
between us.
After passing in the hall
all semester,
I finally came to terms
with knowing you.
Deciding to chug our beers
and search for more,
        maybe even dance
        at the old bar "uptown"
we were off.
Discussing our lives,
as well and the latest on Morrissey,
we delved deeper into
a friendship, our souls,
and so much else.
It takes a lot, you know,
to bare one's soul,
but with you, I knew
it was okay.
And as that night slowly ended,
I felt the meaning that
was in your handshake,
and then I said goodbye...

"Corey (1988)"

I thought about you
this morning

      ...about the all-nighters in the computer lab
      ...about walking home late in the dawn
      ...about how these days, it just isn't the same

and I wondered
what have you been doing lately
and where are you now?

A lost treasure
takes more space in the heart
than one possessed.

Come, bring your pipe Mike,
let's relax once again
to the tune of the old times,
one last time.....

(For Michael K.)

"All-Nighter Memories; B.G.S.U. – 1987"

Today is the day I bury, my son...

I wake before sunrise, my son,
the demons of sleep
still haunting, the ides
of night... restless evermore.

Today is the day I bury, my son,
my task-laden hands
are heavy, my heart
sinks deeper than any grave.

Other mothers' pain, my son,
cannot be known today,
just as my answers to "why"
are carried away on the wind.

Know my son, when you awake
in the morning after life,
it was I who comforted you,
I who covered you in the blankets of the earth.

For today is the day I bury, my son...

"For Toby – 2009"

I could tell you
what the word "friend"
means to me,
or I could tell you
how much of that
friend you've come to be

I could tell you
all of the good times
I've shared with you,
and I could tell you
how much I'm going to
miss those times
when you leave

I could tell you
everyone knows
you'll do fine,
or I could tell you
no matter how things go
I'll still believe in you

I could tell you
my friend
all of this and more,
but sometimes
silence speaks louder than words...

"Dave (1989)"

Parade's in town, my summer friend

Returning once again, you may have heard

In hopes of celebration

Decrying another year of fears

Everyone's invited, one and all

Remnants of glitter, past

Invigorating floats, costumes galore

Dress for the occasion

Everyone's invited, one and all

Ignoring the calculated hate

Days on end, for we're free

Everyone's invited, one and all

Dreary skies no longer hold balloons

Everyone's invited, one and all

Everyone, everything, everywhere…faded away now
   - shouldn't it last all year?

(for Jerry)

"Disappearing PRIDE - everyone's invited"

I remember having the ubiquitous
Farrah Fawcett swimsuit poster
tacked to one bedroom wall of my youth

the four walls being
fortifications against premonitory angst,
painted a gratefully dedicated shade
of ochre-yellow not to be seen again

the poster's colorful blanket background
yes, it was there
now, you remember it
her feathered hair and pervasive smile
hovering above red, Adonis-perfect mammilla

a supposition just right to elicit
lustful feelings in the teenage self

when the actual reality of it all
were only feelings of wondering
why I felt different
from the other boys...

"Not like the other boys"

You made me feel like a whore
that time you gave me $20
in the back of the X-rated movie theater
    the one, only, last time
    I took anything from you:
        from others, many others
        some more, some less
    but no more from you.

We both got what we wanted that day
    to feel human, while making
    the other feel anything but.

    You – a quickie before home
    to the wife, the kids.
    Me – a twenty spot before comfort
    at the carryout, once again.

In darkened spaces, so many pass
    hands, transactions, missed connections;
    and while living to see the light
    of another day, all parties
    must always remain in the shadows
    until we return again.

"Survivalist Transactions"

                                          I remember
                                    playing jump rope
                                 in elementary school,
                       playing hopscotch and four-square...
                            the boys never saying anything,
                                       but always looking
                        with that strange look in their eyes.

I remember
dancing with the girls
at junior-high dances,
dancing always fast, never slow...
the boys never saying anything,
but always looking
with that strange look in their eyes.

                                          I remember
                                    acting in drama club
                                    at the old high school,
                        acting while subconsciously labeled...
                            the boys never saying anything,
                                       but always looking
                        with that strange look in their eyes.

| remember
sharing your bed
after some college party,
moving further rather than closer...
the boys never saying anything,
but always looking
with that strange look in their eyes.

                                          I remember
                                    telling you that day
                                     on your front porch,
                          hugging you for reassurance...
                            the boys never saying anything,
                                       but always looking
                        with that strange look in their eyes.

I don't remember
being tied to the fence
in some rural countryside,
wincing as the hammer strikes me again...
the boys never saying anything,
but always looking
with that strange look in their eyes.

"Gay wad"

I will not be lead to the slaughter...

you stand there with your book in hand
dying in vain to judge my soul
while every day, your world becomes less and less
crumbling into eternity, falling into your own abyss

"Burn in hell!" you say and you shout
while every day, my world becomes a raging inferno
a raging flame of desire, burning within my heart
to seek the knowledge and know why I stand apart

I cannot abide your systems or beliefs
your gods and demons to me are foreign
one can never have faith again
once the faithful have lead you astray...again

I will not be lead to the slaughter
to a bloodbath of the common mind
the masses have their opiates to make them whole
their fixes bought once again by selling their souls

I will not be lead to the slaughter.....

"Jerusa-Lamb"

4

ONE LAST ONE

The

"poem
that
is
a
poem
but
it's
not
really
a
poem
because
it
doesn't
have
a
title
it
just
asks
a
question"

poem…

"Poetry...or art?"

Postscript

We have all lived "100 lives" in this simple lifetime.

And everyone has given up at least one thing in doing so.

Passing through...shedding pasts...this lifetime.

Do you ever ponder the life you gave up....for the life you have?

Something to think about until we read the next time...

Gratitude

To my husband, Joel
Thank you for your ongoing support through this project, through the months and years of me finding my creative pen, and through the decades of being my soul mate. You are the ground control to my lofty ambitions, always encouraging me and always reminding me not to lose my perspective. I "love you more" every single day!

To my Mother and my Sister
As a family unit, we have experienced all manner of life and lifetimes, sometimes even more than one at the same time. And yet, aside from all the mental and physical bruises the universe has shown us, we remain unscathed and stronger than ever in our love and support for each other. "Expect the Unexpected." (Dad) has been a guiding light through this world. He would be proud. Thank you both for your love and support!

To Balboa Press
Thank you to the staff and team working on this second book project with me. While nothing is ever easy, your support and guidance has made this publishing project a wonderful experience. The bumps in the road always become smooth. I am grateful for the working relationship we have and the ease with which this project came to fruition!

To my "Beta Readers"
A few wished not to be mentioned by name, so in respect and with fairness, I express my gratitude to each of you for your feedback, one and all. If you were one, you know who you are. Your insight was not taken lightly and was most helpful during this project.

To Linda F.
Our friendship was short-lived and cut short; the universe apparently had other plans than our regular coffee chats. Our visits made it feel like we knew each other's world inside and out. Yet, in reality,

we hardly even knew each other - we thought we had more time. The energy your smile showed to the world was incapable of being captured by mere mortals remaining here on Earth. It must be needed elsewhere. I certainly hope they truly appreciate it as much as I did, because I sure as hell miss it. "Luv Ya, Gurl!"

And finally, **Thank You Readers.** Once again, you have given your time and made the choice to peruse my words, hopefully finding a brief respite from the daily grind. My gratitude will be forever appreciative and humble.

Printed in the United States
by Baker & Taylor Publisher Services